HISTORIC HOMES of SAN AUGUSTINE

HISTORIC HOMES

Compiled by ANNE CLARK

# of SAN AUGUSTINE

Edited by Carolyn Allen   Photographs by Jim Alvis

1972 / Jointly published by THE SAN AUGUSTINE HISTORICAL SOCIETY and THE ENCINO PRESS / Austin

© 1972 / The Encino Press / 2003 South Lamar / Austin

Typesetting: LUCAS & CLARK / Paper: LONE STAR PAPER COMPANY / Printing: CAPITAL PRINTING COMPANY / Binding: CUSTOM BOOKBINDERS / Design: WILLIAM D. WITTLIFF

To Mama Clark, My Own Amazing Grace

INTRODUCTION

ACCORDING to an old Indian legend, there was once a powerful chief who was the father of two sons, both equally beloved; the problem of heirship seemed insurmountable until one day the chief discovered the answer. He led his two sons to the banks of the river, now known as the Sabine, and said to them, "One of you shall make a day's march to the East, and the other shall make a day's march to the West. At the end of your journey, you shall each establish a village and thenceforth justly rule the people in your domain." Thus it was said that the sister towns of Natchitoches, Louisiana, and Nacogdoches, Texas, had their beginnings.

Later came the French and Spanish to establish trade routes from the Red River to the Spanish possessions in Mexico, thereby displacing the Indians. The rival colonial powers attempted to cement their territorial claims by sending missionaries to work among the Indians, and missions were established which had as their goal political as well as religious conversion of the Indians.

One of these missions—Mission Nuestra Señora de los Dolores de Ais—was situated on the banks of Ayish Bayou, in the settlement of the Aies Indians, just south of the present town of San Augustine. "The King's Highway" or El Camino Real grew into a trading route and along side of it grew the town of San Augustine. Around 1818 settlers from the United States began migrating to Texas and particularly to the Ayish Bayou area. This migration marked the third time that the site of San Augustine was chosen for a permanent settlement—first by the Indians, next the Spanish, and finally Anglo-American settlers.

By 1824, the settlement had a water mill to grind cornmeal and in 1826 a cotton gin. In 1827 the community witnessed its first major dispute—the Fredonian Uprising—a fight over land titles which was forcibly arbitrated at the Battle of Ayish Bayou by Colonel Prather and his men. The settlement's population increased steadily and in 1832 there were enough residents to justify the establishment of a town. The township was laid out by Thomas McFarland, surveyor and early resident, in 1833; by 1834 San Augustine was incorporated. It soon grew in importance and became one of the foremost American colonies in Texas.

In 1836, San Augustine sent as delegates to sign the Texas Declaration of Independence, S. W. Blount and E. O. LeGrand; it also fielded three companies of men to fight in the battle for independence. Through the years San Augustine has furnished many notable men in the civil, military, and judicial ranks of the state including one president, one vice-president, three governors, two lieutenant governors, one Confederate States congressman, three judges of the Supreme Court, six district judges, two generals in the Texas Army and four generals in the Confederate Army.

William Seale in *San Augustine in the Texas Republic* writes that "Architecturally, San Augustine built an environment eminently superior to any town in Texas—with the possible exception of Galveston—prior even to the Civil War. This was largely the contribution of Augustus Phelps, a New England carpenter-architect," and the most talented of a group of contractor-builders including a man named Lovell and T. C. Broocks. In spite of the passing of time, the great fire of 1890, and "progress," many structures have endured unchanged and little dishevelled by the century and a quarter that has passed since the creation of the Republic. An unprecedented number of nineteenth century dwellings have survived. They range in style from fine Greek Revival mansions to dogtrot cottages, and log cabins, with many still in the possession of and occupied by the descendants of the original owners. Raiford Stripling, San Augustine's talented restoration architect, is largely responsible for the renewal of interest and restoration of these old houses—making San Augustine a living museum of Texas in the nineteenth century.

To paraphrase Daniel Webster's famous saying: "San Augustine, sir, is a small town but there are those of us who love it."

ANNE CLARK

CONTENTS

HISTORIC HOMES of SAN AUGUSTINE

MISSION NUESTRA SEÑORA DE LOS DOLORES

(State Highway 147 South, within city of San Augustine)

THE Mission Nuestra Señora de los Dolores de los Ais, or Our Lady of Sorrows, was founded in 1717 to counteract the activities of the French who were by this date well established in Nachitoches. It was the sixth of the East Texas missions and was located in the tribe of the Aies Indians on the banks of Ayish Bayou. The mission appears to be the second oldest settlement within the boundaries of the state of Texas, and it is the first European settlement in the Ayish Bayou Area.

The mission was founded by Padre Antonio Margil de Jesús of the Domingo Ramón expedition to confirm the claim of the king of Spain to the province of Texas and to instruct the Aies Indians in the doctrines of Christianity. When the French invaded the area in 1719, the mission was temporarily abandoned, but later restored in 1721. Nuestra Señora de los Dolores was permanently abandoned in 1773 when the Spanish government ordered the complete abandonment of all East Texas missions and presidios. This event marks the end of the missionary period in East Texas and the beginnings of the struggle for Texas independence from Mexico. A state historical marker on Highway 147, one-half mile south of San Augustine commemorates this mission. The San Augustine Historical Society has purchased this site and plans to rebuild the Jacalie-type mission under the direction of Raiford Stripling, who also restored La Bahía at Goliad.

HENDERSON

JAMES PINCKNEY HENDERSON

JAMES PINCKNEY HENDERSON (1801-1858) whose sculptured image sits high above the sidewalks on the courthouse square, looks serenely down on the state and town he helped to create.

General Henderson came to Texas from North Carolina, arriving in the spring of 1836, when Texas was in the struggle for her independence. He served the Republic and the state of Texas as brigadier general, secretary of state, ambassador to England and France, architect of the Treaty of Annexation, governor, and United States senator. When not in service to his state, General Henderson resided in San Augustine where he practiced law.

While serving as Envoy Extraordinaire to France, General Henderson met Miss Frances Cox in Paris; they were married in 1839 and returned to San Augustine in 1840. A handsome colonial house (now unfortunately demolished), was erected by Henderson in the southern part of town.

George L. Crocket writes: "The Henderson home soon became the chief center of social affairs in the town. Mrs. Henderson, with remarkable tact and courtesy, entertained by turns almost every woman and child in the vicinity, while her husband brought home with him from time to time a brilliant company of the ablest and most learned men in the country.

"Undoubtedly the memory of General Henderson, diplomatist, jurist, soldier, and statesman, deserves to be cherished in any history of the town. Few among her citizens have done as much as he to make its name to be known throughout the borders of the State.

"The public career of General Henderson was one of the cleanest and purest that was ever presented before the people of this country. San Augustine may well be proud that her great citizen has left behind him a record so bright and stainless."

McFARLAND HOUSE
(7 miles west on State Highway 21)

THOMAS S. McFARLAND was born in Indiana in 1810; he came to Texas from Louisiana in 1830. In 1832, McFarland served as aide-de-camp to General James Whitis Bullock in the Battle of Nacogdoches. (This battle resulted in the expulsion of the forces of the Mexican commandant, José de las Piedras.) McFarland also participated in the Siege of Bexar in 1835, and in 1837 was elected lieutenant colonel of the militia at San Augustine.

The town of San Augustine was built upon a tract of 640 acres of land which McFarland purchased from Chichester Chaplin for $200. In 1833, McFarland surveyed and laid out the town of San Augustine on this land. A surveyor by profession, he also laid out the towns of Belgrade and Pendleton.

McFarland later became a leading citizen of San Augustine. He represented Jasper and Jefferson counties in the Senate of the Sixth Congress of the Republic and served three terms as chief justice of San Augustine County. McFarland's father, William, was also a renowned citizen of San Augustine. William accompanied his son to Texas in 1830, participated in the Battle of Nacogdoches, and also represented the Ayish Bayou district in the Conventions of 1832-1833. In 1837, Sam Houston appointed him chief justice of San Augustine County. He served as first worshipful master of McFarland Lodge (later renamed Red Land Lodge), the third Masonic Lodge established in Texas.

The home from which he operated the plantation he had established was located on the south side of the Old San Antonio Road, seven miles west of San Augustine. It was built about the time of the Texas Revolution and was still standing in good condition in 1940.

The house was torn down in 1940 and a four-room house built from the original lumber. The chimney to this house is constructed from the original chimneys. Mr. Walter H. Smith

bought this house and fifty acres of land in 1940. He has since remodeled the house, adding three rooms and a porch, and he resides there at present.

The Texas Centennial Commission of 1936 put up a marker at this house commemorating its historic significance.

THE MILTON GARRETT HOME
(11 miles west on State Highway 21)

MILTON AND WILLIAM were the two sons of Jacob Garrett, a prominent member of the pre-Republic San Augustine community and an early settler in the Ayish Bayou area.

William Garrett came to San Augustine first, followed by his father, Jacob, and Jacob's second son, Milton. Milton Garrett settled on a place overlooking the rich Attoyac River bottomlands, which were later to become the plantations of the Garrett family.

In 1826, Milton built a hand-hewn log house with two stonecut chimneys, one at each end. It is the oldest existing house in San Augustine County and one of the few houses which stands, without additions, as it was originally built. The house is 18 X 30 feet with porches on the back and front, and an interesting cedar balustered stair to the attic room.

The Milton Garrett house is a fine example of native pre-Republic architecture, and one of the few remaining all log houses in the East Texas area. It is now owned and occupied by Raiford Stripling, restoration architect, who has completely restored it.

CAPTAIN T. W. BLOUNT HOUSE
(2½ miles west on State Highway 21)

THE HILL where the Captain T. W. Blount house stands was originally settled in 1822 by John A. Williams, who built one of the first cotton gins in Texas on this site. Jonas Hail later erected a house upon the same site and lived in it until his death. After the Civil War the house was purchased by Captain T. W. Blount. The Blount house, located on the Old San Antonio Road about four miles from San Augustine, is a two-story frame house with an ell containing a kitchen and cooking fireplace.

As an infant, Thomas William Blount came to Texas from Alabama. He later graduated from Kentucky Military Institute and then began to study law. *The Handbook of Texas* summarizes his career: "He was admitted to the bar but preferred plantation life to practicing law. In March, 1861, he was commissioned a Captain in the Confederate Army. He served with General Braxton Braggs in the quartermaster's department and with General A. H. Gladders as aide-de-camp. In 1862, Blount was placed in charge of a battery of engineers and supervised the building of defenses in Mobile Bay. He acted temporarily as chief of ordnance, commanded a battery at Fort Pillon and served with Earl Van Dorn as assistant officer of exchange of prisoners at Vicksburg. In July, 1863, he was captured at Port Hudson and remained a prisoner at Johnson's Island until the end of the War. Parolled on July 12, 1865, he returned to San Augustine on July 4. In 1866, he was elected to represent the Fifth District in the Eleventh Texas Legislature.

"Blount married Mary Rather of Shelby County and was the father of four children. In 1910, he moved into San Augustine, where he died in 1934."

The Captain Blount house is owned by Tom B. Blount of San Augustine, a grandson of the Captain, and the Captain's great-grandchildren, John Seale of Jasper, and Mrs. Betty Blount Wood of Houston.

THE WADE HOUSE—"HOSPITALITY HOUSE"
(Farm Road 705, 12 miles south of San Augustine)

THOMAS SEBASTIAN CABOT WADE, the original owner of the Wade house, and half-brother of E. O. Legrand, a signer of the Texas Declaration of Independence, came from Norwood, North Carolina, and settled about twelve miles south of the town of San Augustine in 1837. Wade was a farmer, a cotton gin and grist mill operator, as well as an owner of a mercantile store located in a hand-hewn log building across the road from the house.

The Wade house was also known as "Hospitality House," a name well earned, for many people enjoyed the Wade hospitality over the years. Men on hunting trips, returning church goers, and those who came to purchase annual supplies, to bring cotton to the gin, or to grind corn could come to the Wades to spend the night, or at least to eat a meal with the family. It is said that "Baptist Pallets" were spread for sleeping, and that there were bowls of sausages, fresh churned butter, fried chicken, and huge pans of fluffy white biscuits.

Before his death, T. S. C. Wade divided the homestead equally among his eight children. Later William Marion Wade, the oldest son of T. S. C. Wade, bought the shares of his seven brothers and sisters in order that the homestead remain intact. He operated the homeplace, which he called the Bar-W Ranch, until his death in 1961. His only son, Nelsyn Ernest Brooks Wade, is now running the cattle and ranch business and owns the Wade house.

The double-pen house, with detached kitchen, was remodeled and restored in 1962 by Mrs. W. M. Wade. Lumber from another 100-year-old house was used for the remodeling. The open hall was enclosed, connecting the kitchen to the house.

ANDERSON—JOHNSON—TEEL HOUSE
(End of North Congress Street)

THE house east of the cemetery, known most commonly as the "Anderson Place" was built by Almanzon Huston in 1838. It is said that the house was financed by James C. Anderson, who at the time planned a new and different home of his own. In 1841, however, he bought this place from Huston, and resided there until his death. It then became the property of his son-in-law, C. C. Johnson, whose grandson, W. J. Teel, now lives there.

Mr. Teel, San Augustine County Judge, has furnished some fascinating historical detail concerning the house: "As mentioned before, the house was actually built by A. Huston (think Mr. Huston operated one of the early hotels in San Augustine.) J. C. Anderson had a temporary home on the southwest shelf of the large hill located about ½ mile NW of this location . . . (he) planned to build a permanent home on top of this hill but as indicated above, he made a trade with Mr. Huston and bought this place. In this connection, it might be pointed out that the City Cemetery located West of the house was the family cemetery. Other people were allowed to use it and later two or three families bought small sections. The Anderson-Johnson-Teel graves are located near the crest of the slight hill and the Anderson slaves were buried to the southwest. . . .

"Many, many guests have been entertained in this house. Other than family and relatives, itinerant politicians, people attending court, and ministers of all faiths. The family was Scottish Presbyterian but it was known that any minister would be cared for there. The story is that a minister of a group who only had a few members in San Augustine at the time was in Nacogdoches and planning to come to San Augustine. He was told to go to the Anderson place, for he would be welcome and cared for. This he was and they found a place for him to preach and sent word around that he would preach at a certain time. When all assembled, he preached a sermon in which he told them all they were going to hell because they were not in his church. They were amused but he was still welcome."

Mr. Teel has also supplied some information concerning the points of architectural interest in the house: "So far as we know, all of the materials are local in origin. The sills and frame work seem to be oak, hand-hewn, mortised and pegged. Almost everything else is long leaf pine. The most interesting features of the house are the panelled "presses" (closets), covering the entire west wall of the main bedroom. There are four upper and four lower "presses," four on each side of the fireplace. Another unusual feature is the recessed chimney; the first story section is exposed and flush with the outside wall, with the second story part entirely covered."

At present, the house is owned by W. J. Teel of San Augustine.

COLUMBUS CARTWRIGHT HOUSE
(203 West Main)

COLUMBUS CARTWRIGHT was the son of Matthew Cartwright, one of the first settlers in the San Augustine area. He was a prestigious, well-respected man in the San Augustine community, and a devoted member of the Methodist Church. In 1897, Cartwright donated an entire block of land in front of the church to the congregation, and a large parsonage was erected there. In 1907 the old church site was abandoned and sold; a new church of artificial stone was built on the land.

The Columbus Cartwright house was built in 1838. This date, now eroded, was reputedly carved on one of the old chimneys of the house. The house was added to by the moving of the Bailey Anderson house as an attachment to the south side. The house is one and one-half stories, originally with a back hall to the stairway. The Columbus Cartwright house has been restored by architect Raiford Stripling, with carpenter work done by Ray Bennefield and Louis Runnels. It is presently owned and lived in by Thelma and Winnie Nicholson of San Augustine.

THE BOB McCAULEY HOUSE
(8 miles northwest on Farm Road 711, northeast 6 miles)

THE original headright of the tract of land on which the Bob McCauley house is located was made to James McCauley, grandfather of Bob McCauley, in 1838. James McCauley's brother, John, built the first house on the tract with the help of his slaves. The one-room house and outbuildings were made of hewn logs. Later Bob McCauley remodeled the house making the north wing from the original structure and enclosing the log room with sheet rock, hiding the original logs.

The design of the porch is unique, having profile columns on the rear of the house which have been cut from four by eights. The house is presently owned by the heirs of Mrs. R. C. McCauley, and is occupied by Mrs. E. B. Bittick, one of the McCauley heirs.

EZEKIEL CULLEN HOUSE
(205 South Congress)

THE OUTSTANDING architectural feature of the Judge Ezekiel W. Cullen home, built in 1839 by the master builder, Augustus Phelps, is the use of the Texas Star which is centered over the double door molding, and also the downspouts at either end of the porch. Doric columns support the porch gable and interesting panel decorations, usually seen only in interiors, surround the windows. The garret of the house was finished as a ballroom, extending the entire length of the house. There are fan-shaped windows at each end of the ballroom which open today just as they did 125 years ago. The simple one-story Greek Revival style house is one of the loveliest of its type standing in Texas today.

At some date prior to 1835, Ezekiel Cullen left Georgia with a law degree, ten thousand dollars and a body servant to come to Texas; he soon became one of the most prominent citizens of the new Republic. Mrs. Cullen, who people said was "a woman possessing all of the charm and refinement of a true daughter of the Old South," left her home in Mississippi to accompany her husband to Texas.

After settling in San Augustine, Cullen began practicing law as an active member of the San Augustine bar association from 1837 to 1848. He was a member of the third Congress of the Texas Republic in 1838-39, and represented San Augustine in the House. Cullen was appointed judge of the First Judicial District and associate justice of the Supreme Court of the Republic of Texas. Judge Cullen, as a member of Congress, was author of the bill setting aside public lands for the support of public education and for the University of Texas and Texas A&M. In 1850, President Zachary Taylor appointed Cullen purser of the U. S. Navy, and he left San Augustine for the next twenty years to fulfill the duties of this position.

After the Civil War, the Cullen house became the property of the Elisha Roberts family. After returning from his federal post in Washington, D. C., in 1871 Judge Cullen moved to Dallas. He died in 1874.

In 1952, Hugh Roy Cullen, grandson of Judge Cullen, purchased the property and commissioned the noted restoration architect, Raiford Stripling, to restore the structure. He employed Louis Runnels and Ray Bennefield as carpenters. After a very costly restoration, Mr. and Mrs. Cullen presented the house to the Ezekiel Cullen Chapter of the Daughters of the Republic of Texas in 1953. The Ezekiel Cullen House is listed on the National Register of Historic Places, U. S. Department of the Interior, National Park Service.

EZEKIEL CULLEN HOUSE

THE OLD GREER HOUSE
(Junction of US Highway 96 and Farm Road 1277)

THE GREER HOUSE was originally a one-room frame cabin built by Charleton Payne, a business partner of Thomas Napoleon Bonaparte Greer. Raiford Stripling, San Augustine's restoration architect, has identified the workmanship of the moldings on the house as being that of Augustus Phelps at a . date between 1838 and 1842. Thomas N. B. Greer acquired the land sometime shortly after the Texas Revolution.

Greer, born in Tennessee in 1808, was the brother of John Alexander Greer and one of the sixteen children of Thomas and Rebecca Greer. He immigrated to Texas in 1835, and enlisted in the Texas Army as a private in the regular artillery. He participated in the Battle of San Jacinto and was honorably discharged in June, 1836. According to *The Handbook of Texas* it was in February of 1840 that "he raised a company of Boggy and Trinity Rangers under commission of Mirabeau B. Lamar. Greer was killed by Indian marauders on the Trinity River in Houston County in June, 1842." Raiford Stripling did the restoration of the old Greer house. Mrs. Ben Harwit of Midland is the present owner of the house.

MATTHEW CARTWRIGHT HOUSE
(912 Main Street)

THE MATTHEW CARTWRIGHT house in San Augustine is one of the finest early examples of the Greek Revival style of architecture; the house is significant for its handsome proportions, bold entablature, and sophisticated, yet restrained use of Greek Revival details. The house is also renowned as the home of two early Texas pioneers who took active parts in establishing the Republic.

The house was built in 1839 for Isaac Campbell by the master builder, Augustus Phelps, and was located directly across the street from San Augustine University, which later merged with Wesleyan College to form the University of Eastern Texas. Campbell, who was one of the committee that selected the site for the capital city of Austin, moved from San Augustine a short time later, and the building was used temporarily for classes of Wesleyan College until its permanent building was completed. Information from the National Register of Historic Places states: "It is traditionally held that Augustus Phelps' workmen were unable to solve the problem of the narrow winding stair in the house, and General T. C. Broocks, another of the three master builders in San Augustine, was engaged to construct the stair. Several of the outbuildings on the property are as carefully designed as the main structure.

Matthew Cartwright participated in the Siege of Bexar and the Battle of Concepción and was a cavalryman at San Jacinto (his horse was shot out from under him the day before the battle).

In 1847, Cartwright purchased the Isaac Campbell residence; his wife, Amanda Holman Cartwright, was Isaac Campbell's sister-in-law. The Cartwright family, coming from Tennessee, were among the first settlers in the area during the 1820s. Cartwright's father, John, built three stores in San Augustine and named his sons as managers; Matthew managed two of these stores, but amassed his own fortune by recognizing the value of buying land in unsettled areas of Texas. Cartwright lived in the residence until his death in the 1870s, and the house has remained in the possession of his descendants.

Mrs. Mintie Cartwright Kardell and her husband, Steve Kardell, reside in and are the present owners of the house.

The Matthew Cartwright house is listed on the National Register of Historic Places, U. S. Department of the Interior, National Park Service.

THE STEPHEN W. BLOUNT HOUSE
(501 East Columbia)

COLONEL STEPHEN WILLIAM BLOUNT came to Texas from Georgia by way of Alabama and Louisiana. His father and grandfather bore the same name before him, the latter having served in the American Revolutionary War.

In the summer of 1835, while on business in Montgomery, Alabama, Colonel Blount met a man from Nacogdoches, who gave him such a glowing description of Texas that he decided to migrate there at once. On the trip, coming through Louisiana, Blount learned from some wagoners that there was a famine of salt meat in San Augustine, Texas. After buying a wagonload of bacon, he proceeded to San Augustine and sold the bacon at a small profit, thus giving evidence on his first arrival of the business enterprise and public spirit which were marked characteristics of his entire life.

Colonel Blount settled in San Augustine and was, from the beginning, an ardent advocate of Texas independence. In January, 1836, he was chosen as a delegate to the convention at Washington on the Brazos, where he was one of the signers of the Declaration of Independence on March 2, 1836. In 1846, Blount was elected clerk of the county court when San Augustine County was organized. He was a faithful and indefatigable officer and also served as postmaster for several years in the small community. All through his life he was industriously engaged in the mercantile business, while attaining for himself a reputation for generosity and shrewdness with his customers.

Colonel Blount died in 1890 at the age of 82; his physical condition and spirit at the end attested to his remarkable energy throughout his life. He is buried in the City Cemetery of San Augustine.

Colonel Blount's home in San Augustine exemplifies the spirit of the man. Built in 1839 on the corner of Columbia and Ayish streets, the home, which was constructed by Augustus Phelps and restored by Raiford Stripling, is considered one of the finest examples of Greek Revival architecture in the South. The house is one story, finely proportioned and beautifully ornamented. The porch, supported by fluted Doric columns, is the outstanding feature of the house from the exterior. The home is a fitting landmark to one of Texas' spirited pioneers.

The Stephen W. Blount house is owned by Ray R. Stripling of San Augustine, and was restored by his father, Raiford Stripling.

THE POLK HOUSE
(717 West Columbia Street)

THE Polk house was built in 1840 for Ransom H. Horn by Horn and his brother F. N. Horn, an early cabinet and furniture maker in San Augustine. F. N. Horn purchased the tools of the master builder Augustus Phelps, and later became a famous carpenter in his own right.

Mr. Will Partin of San Augustine, a great-grandson of Ransom H. Horn, says that he and F. N. Horn and W. H. Horn were brothers and all worked together around the same time. There are several fascinating vignettes concerning the Horn family.

While still a boy, Mr. F. N. Horn had a great fancy for John Polk and called himself by this name; he was accordingly known all his life as "John Horn," although he signed his name "F. N. Horn."

Mr. Ransom Horn, called Uncle Ransom, was a prominent member of the Methodist Church. His unofficial function in the church was to "raise the tunes" to the hymns—that is, to give the pitch to the congregation, as they had no organs or hymnals in the church. When the first organ was installed in the church, Mr. Horn withdrew his services as leader, refusing to have anything to do with the "four-footed beast." A window in the present Methodist Church commemorates him as a "great and good man."

Still another story concerning the Horn family relates that on a cold, stormy winter evening a child was abandoned on the gatepost of the Horn residence. When someone came out of the house and found the orphaned child in such a peculiar place, he was nicknamed "Gatepost Horn" and was forever after known by this sobriquet.

R. H. Horn's house was later purchased by Harry K. Polk, grandson of Judge Alfred Polk, a man who was prominent in local affairs in the pre-Civil War period. The house itself is a clapboard, one-story structure with double front wings, a wide central hall, shed rooms and an attached kitchen. The construction of the entrance doorway and mantels is particularly interesting. The house also furnishes the only remaining example of painted decorations in the area.

Raiford Stripling, the restoration architect, supervised the design and reconstruction of this house; Ray Bennefield and Louis Runnels were the carpenters.

Mrs. Kate Polk Gillian is the present owner and resides in the house.

MEMORIAL PRESBYTERIAN CHURCH
(East Livingston Street)

THE MEMORIAL PRESBYTERIAN CHURCH was organized by the Reverend Hugh Wilson, D. D., on June 2, 1838. A great many of the members today are descended from the charter members, of which there were originally 22, including two slaves. The first site of the church, then named Bethel Presbyterian Church, was Goodlaw's schoolhouse four miles west of San Augustine. In 1840, the members moved the church into San Augustine, and it became the San Augustine Presbyterian Church. On the occasion of the 50th Anniversary of the church in 1887, it was renamed Memorial Presbyterian Church in honor of the charter members.

Reverend D. A. McRae, organizer of the McRae Presbyterian Church, and a devoted minister, was pastor from 1880 until his death in 1920. In the sanctuary there are three pulpit chairs dating back to the erection of the building, two of the original handmade pews, and a copy of the original Session Records. The church has no ornamentation, neither within nor on the outside, in keeping with the austerity of the Calvinist tradition.

On the 129th anniversary of Memorial Presbyterian Church its congregation made the following dedication: "Memorial Presbyterian Church stands in memory and prayerful dedication to the early pioneers who organized the first Presbyterian Church in Texas."

DR. B. F. SHARP—"CHINA GROVE"
(5 miles northwest off US Highway 96)

DR. B. F. SHARP, one of the sons of M. D. L. Sharp, settled in San Augustine about 1848. He bought the house, later known as "China Grove," from S. S. Davis, who served with the volunteers during the Texas Revolution, was a representative at the Fourth Congress, and later was sheriff of San Augustine County. Davis received the house in the will of A. M. Davis, who purchased the place from Edmond Chinith, grandson of Edmond Quirk. Quirk received title to a ten league grant from Antonio Leal in 1801; part of this grant is the land upon which the town of San Augustine was built. Dr. B. F. Sharp and his bride, the former Martha Ann Hall, daughter of the governor of Tennessee took up their residency in the old Davis place. Mrs. Sharp named it "China Grove" plantation because of the great number of China trees growing around it. Originally the plantation contained 900 acres, but at present, it includes only 410 acres. Mrs. Sally Sharp Hall was the fourth generation Sharp to own "China Grove"; her daughter Mrs. Anne Hall King of Tyler, now owns it. The "China Grove" house is constructed of large square hand-hewn logs and has four rooms, two large ones behind, with a hallway extending the entire length. The original chimneys, one on each end, are made of hand-hewn rock. Inside are two beautiful pine mantels.

THE OLD POLK OR SHARP HOUSE
(7 miles southwest on Farm Road 1277, then 2 miles east)

THE house known as the old Polk or Sharp house was originally built around 1845, by Augustus Phelps, San Augustine's master builder. In 1852, Lucius B. Polk, son of the famed "fighting Bishop," the Confederate General Polk, bought 500 acres of land in the Augustus Phelps survey, including the house Phelps built. Lucius Polk enlarged the house and later willed it to his daughter, Mrs. Mollie Sharp Polk, who married B. F. Sharp, grandson of M. D. L. Sharp and son of Dr. James Sharp. As a result of this marriage the house came to be known as the Polk-Sharp house.

An interesting feature of this place is a smokehouse built of heart pine in the rear of the main house to help provide the extra food necessary for the slaves. The smokehouse is a two-story structure with the steps built inside the house. Lucius Polk dried beef in the upper part and smoked pork in the lower floor.

The main house has fine stone-cut chimneys, a molded entranceway, and twenty-four 8-light glass windows. The house is now owned by the heirs of Mrs. Mollie Sharp Polk.

THE CROCKET HOUSE
(Market and Ayish Street)

GEORGE LOUIS CROCKET, author of *Two Centuries in East Texas*, was known as the "grand old man of East Texas"— he was a churchman, scholar, historian, humanitarian, and craftsman. Mr. Crocket was born in a two-room house in San Augustine, June 3, 1861, the youngest of five children of George Fulton Crocket and Elmira Louisa Sharp Crocket. After completing his education in the public schools of San Augustine and at the University of the South in Tennessee, Mr. Crocket served as rector of the Episcopal Church in San Augustine for forty-two years, and as part-time rector in Nacogdoches for twenty-four years. He also did missionary work in Lufkin, Corrigan, Garrison, New Birmingham, and Center. In 1929, Mr. Crocket became Professor Emeritus of History at Stephen F. Austin State Teachers College in Nacogdoches, where he collected and organized data relating to the history of East Texas. This he published in his book entitled *Two Centuries in East Texas*, a definitive history of East Texas as well as a history of the beginnings of the state. He knew more about the history of this area than any other man and wrote of it in a scholarly, well-organized manner. George Crocket died January 3, 1936, in Nacogdoches.

Mr. Crocket's pen-and-ink sketches are preserved in the Archives Collection at the University of Texas, and his original maps and charts were bequeathed to Stephen F. Austin State College at Nacogdoches.

The Crocket house was built in 1845 by Dr. Samuel Sexton, father of Colonel F. B. Sexton. There is a beautiful mantel in the parlor; and the house itself is an interesting combination of two-story, story and a half, and one-story addition. Tom B. Blount and Mrs. Betty Blount Wood of Houston, and John Seale of Jasper are the present owners of the Crocket house.

"PET" SHARP HOUSE
(507 Congress Street)

Lafayette Sharp (also known as Pet Sharp) was the grandson of M. D. L. Sharp, early Texas settler, and the son of Dr. B. F. Sharp, owner of China Grove Plantation. Lafayette Sharp is also the father of Mr. Willie Sharp, Sublett Sharp, and Mrs. Kate Sharp McMillan, and the grandfather of Charles Sharp McMillan.

In 1884, Lafayette Sharp purchased the house now known as the Pet Sharp house from W. H. Horn, brother of F. N. and R. H. Horn. Structural evidence identifies certain features of the house as being built by W. H. Horn and F. N. Horn, early carpenters and cabinetmakers in San Augustine. Apparently F. N. Horn also helped build the Polk house, as the style of construction in both homes is similar.

The Pet Sharp house was constructed around 1850 and was originally located across Columbia Street from the old Masonic Lodge building. The porch railings and columns were lost in moving the house to its present location. It is now owned by Mrs. Atmar (Gladys Baker) Stanford.

THE MOTT HOUSE
(Near intersection of US Highway 96 and Angelina River)

THE MOTT HOUSE, built at Zavalla / Angelina County, Texas, in the fall of 1852 by Colonel T. L. Mott, was nearly destroyed ten years ago when the McGee Bend Dam, then being constructed, threatened to cover the cabin with water. But Mrs. Bennie Polk Morgan, a kinsman, came to the rescue by acquiring the old Mott house and moving it to a hilltop safely above the waterline. She furnished the cabin with furniture of the early Texas period and also had a log, double-pen corncrib moved with the house.

Thomas Leonard Mott, the builder of the cabin, came to Texas from Mississippi, where he had served as a colonel in the Twenty-third Regiment of the Mississippi Militia in 1838. His four-room cottage of ax-hewn pine and cypress shingles was built in the Concord Community, not far from the Angelina River in the southeast part of Angelina County. The house at first had only two rooms, but Mott later added a lean-to construction which expanded the house to four rooms. One of these new rooms served for a time as post office for that section of the county. Colonel Mott was postmaster for the settlement of Mott in 1871. He died in 1878, but the cabin, with its square-headed nails, original beams, wooden-peg hinges and stone fireplace, has endured the years. Its present owner is Mrs. Bronson (Bennie Polk) Morgan of Jasper.

WILLIAM GARRETT PLANTATION HOUSE
(1 mile west on State Highway 21)

IN December 1854, Mary Garrett wrote home to Texas from New Jersey, where she had been sent to school: ". . . This is a very lonesum place although there is so many girls. . . . Pa, you must be sure and come after me. . . . Just to think of HOME that sweet place home pa you do not know how much we suffer here it is so hard for us to stay. . . . You must excuse all mistakes and the bad writing and write immediately to your daughter."

The letter was written to William Garrett, who originally started a mercantile business in Nacogdoches and then moved to Ayish Bayou and finally settled west of San Augustine. According to Dorothy Bracken, author of *Early Texas Homes*, "In 1861 he built a house there of such proportions that it might have been patterned after his homesick daughter's dream."

It is reported that in the building of the house "Garrett's slaves carefully selected timbers from the virgin pine forest that surrounded the hallowed ground upon which the house was to be built. After many months of planing the lumber, molding the nails and constructing a foundation of timbers joined with pegs, construction of the house was begun. However, it was not until sometime in 1864 that the last nail had been driven and the last pane of glass inserted into the window."

As described in *Early Texas Homes*, the plantation house has a double-entrance doorway flanked "by sidelights the width of the doors themselves. The dormers in the roof are oversized as are the twelve-light windows of the first floor. In every detail of its appearance the house is broad and welcoming and homelike."

William Garrett's father, Jacob Garrett, followed him to Texas from Arkansas and Tennessee. Jacob Garrett acquired a land-grant on the Attoyac River which became, in later years, one of the largest plantations in the country. Still later, Garrett purchased and resided in the Thomas McFarland home, seven miles west of San Augustine. Jacob Garrett was a prominent figure in the birth of the Texas Republic. He was a delegate to the first convention which met in 1832 at San Felipe to petition the Mexican government for the redress of numerous grievances, a member of the Consultation which in 1835 created a provisional Texas government, and a representative from San Augustine in the Permanent Council.

In 1934, the Library of Congress commissioned an architect to prepare blueprints of the exact layout of the house. After completion, these blueprints were placed in the Library so that the historical nature and architecture of the house might be preserved for future generations.

Horticulturists will take note of the chinaberry tree with a cedar tree growing from one of its branches, which is located at the southwest corner of the house.

The Garrett family cemetery is located one-fourth mile to the northeast of the house, but it is not open to the public.

Mr. and Mrs. Cornell T. Dorsey of San Augustine are the present owners of the William Garrett plantation house.

THE COLONEL SEXTON HOUSE
(In New Hope Community, 8 miles NW off State Highway 21)

THE COLONEL SEXTON HOUSE in San Augustine was built by Colonel Franklin B. Sexton in 1861. Sexton was born in Indiana, July 28, 1828, but moved to Texas with his parents at an early age. He attended Wesleyan College and later received his legal training from the eminent lawyers then in San Augustine.

In 1861, shortly after he entered the Confederate Army, Colonel Sexton was elected to a vacancy in the Texas Senate, but returned to Texas too late to take his seat. Subsequently, in November, 1861, Colonel Sexton was elected Texas representative in the House of Representatives to the Congress of the Confederacy. During the war, he spent most of his time in Richmond participating in the legislative decisions of that body.

Returning to San Augustine after the war, Colonel Sexton maintained his home there for several years, later moving to Marshall, Texas. Throughout his life, Sexton was very active in Texas Masonic activities, being elected Grand Commander of the Knights-Templar of Texas in 1870. Colonel Sexton died at the home of his daughter, May 15, 1900, in El Paso, Texas.

Professor George L. Crocket in *Two Centuries in East Texas*, writes of Sexton: "he was a Christian gentleman of the highest character . . . an able and conscientious lawyer, and a sound, conservative statesman. While he was lacking in that personal attraction which wins the multitude, his popularity was based upon the sterling qualities of manhood which confer a lasting reputation."

Mr. and Mrs. Leslie R. Smith are the present owners of the Colonel Sexton house.

44

CHRIST CHURCH
(Ayish Street)

SAN AUGUSTINE'S CHRIST CHURCH, "mother church' to Episcopal churches in Lufkin, Nacogdoches, Center, Marshall, Palestine, and other places, was founded in 1848 by Reverend Henry Samson. It is one of five charter churches in the Diocese of Texas. The establishment of the church came about through the perseverance of Mrs. James Pinckney Henderson, wife of Governor J. P. Henderson, first governor of the state of Texas. Mrs. Henderson wrote repeatedly to Philadelphia to the Committee on Domestic Missions of the Episcopal Church requesting that a missionary be sent to East Texas. Finally, the Reverend Henry Samson was sent in April, 1848, to do missionary work in San Augustine. The Christ Church documents relate an incident which occurred at the beginning of Reverend Samson's ministry: "Mr. Samson's first service was the burial of his oldest child, who died of scarlet fever the day after the family arrived in San Augustine. The child's remains are interred under the church altar."

In 1851, three years after the founding of the church, a brick, Gothic style church building was constructed. In 1859, the church was destroyed by a storm, and with it were lost the stained-glass windows and organ. In 1869, a movement was started to build a new church. The father of George L. Crocket, author of *Two Centuries in East Texas*, and rector of Christ Church for 41 years, donated the land, and Colonel Stephen W. Blount donated the lumber and shingles. Determined that this building would withstand the weathering process of storms and time, the builders used boxed walls thoroughly braced on both sides. On Christmas, 1870, the first service was held in the new building, which has been in constant use since.

Many talented ministers including the Reverend R. D. Shindler, the Reverend Joseph Cross, and the Reverend George L. Crocket have served the church.

In the church today one can see the original rails and hand-hewn pews and the lovely carvings done by George Crocket's own hand. Christ Church was restored by San Augustine restoration artist, Raiford Stripling.

NORWOOD—LEGRAND HOUSE
(Farm Road 705, 12 miles south of San Augustine)

THE OLD NORWOOD HOME was built somewhere between 1865 and 1875 by James L. Norwood and his wife, Emily Fox. James Norwood's parents, William C. Norwood and Eliza Legrand, sister of E. O. Legrand, one of the signers of the Texas Declaration of Independence, came to Texas in 1847 and built a home on Turkey Creek in what is now known as Norwood about ten miles south of San Augustine. E. O. Legrand was not only one of the original signers of the Texas Declaration of Independence, but he also served as a delegate to the convention at Washington-on-the-Brazos, fought at the Battle of San Jacinto, and later served as chief justice of San Augustine County. Legrand never married but made his home with his brother, James B. Legrand, and his brother-in-law, W. C. Norwood.

The house was originally built with an upstairs balcony opening out from the upstairs ballroom. There were five fireplaces, one in each end of the upstairs ballroom, two downstairs and one in the kitchen. The kitchen and dining room were built away from the main house and separated by a dogtrot.

Several years ago, Mrs. W. M. Wade purchased and moved the house to the T. S. C. Wade property on Farm Road 705, twelve miles south of San Augustine. She has restored the main part of the house.

HILLCREST—DR. CURTIS HALEY
(1305 Main Street)

THE HILLCREST ESTATE, lying east of San Augustine on 450 acres of land, was originally owned and built by Professor William R. Leonard. Dr. Leonard built the first part of the house in 1872 and later sold it to Leonidas Cartwright (son of Matthew Cartwright). Cartwright enlarged the house to twelve rooms in 1878 and reared his children there until 1910, when Willie Sharp purchased the house. Mr. Sharp lived in the house until the late 1940s. The present owners are Dr. and Mrs. Curtis Haley, who purchased the estate in January, 1957.

Dr. Haley's description of the home and the estate is most informative: "The house . . . is fronted on the north by a porch extending across the width of the house. A hall extends through the house, but can be closed off in three sections. The home is furnished throughout with antique furniture; it has early Victorian detail, the north portion being a story and a half which is supported by six columns that lend beauty and charm to the home's appearance. The timber was cut locally and the floors are of 1½ inch thick heart pine. The home is unique in that it has seven fireplaces, two of them being upstairs. Several of the fireplace mantels are of marble that reportedly came from France by boat, up the Sabine River to Pendleton and thence to San Augustine. The timbers are hand-hewn and the floors and ceiling boards are hand-planed. The brick were made locally at the old Ayish Bayou brick kiln. Of interest are the two large maple trees in front of the house, that were transplanted by Professor Leonard when he occupied the house. East of the yard is a pecan orchard of 350 trees set out by Willie Sharp in 1912."

PHILLIP A. SUBLETT HOUSE
(State Highway 21, 4 miles east of San Augustine)

PHILLIP SUBLETT was born in Kentucky in 1802; he came to Texas in 1828 and was granted citizenship by the ayuntamiento of Nacogdoches. Sublett purchased the cabin and land of a squatter east of San Augustine and later made additions to the house which he lived in until his death. Phillip Sublett was an active participant in the battle for Texas independence; he was a close friend of Sam Houston and chairman of the Committee of Vigilance and Safety for San Augustine, which in 1835 appointed Sam Houston general and commander in chief of the forces of the department, vesting him with the full powers to raise troops, organize the forces and do all other things appertaining to such office.

When Houston called for volunteers to fight against General Cós at San Antonio, eighty men under the command of Colonel Phillip Sublett rose to the occasion and distinguished themselves in battle. They fought, in the words of George Crocket, "like veterans, from house to house, into the heart of San Antonio," helping to force the unconditional surrender of the Mexican Army.

On August 15, 1836, Sublett nominated Sam Houston for the presidency of the Republic of Texas, and soon after, he and Houston became partners in several land deals. Phillip Sublett died in 1846 at his home in San Augustine.

The present Sublett home, built in 1874, remains in good condition. In *Early Texas Homes* it is described as, "a commodious structure with a long ell running to the rear. The general arrangement of the house is typical of the period in which it was constructed, the two end chimneys serving both lower and upper floors. The entrance door is distinguished by an attractive decorative moulding."

Henry Sublett, great-grandson of Phillip Sublett, lives in and owns the Sublett house.

STRADDLEFORK FARM OR HERRING HOUSE
(7 miles south on Farm Road 705)

STRADDLEFORK FARM is the home of the former ambassador to Australia, Edward Clark and his wife, Anne Clark. In 1965, they purchased the home known as the old Herring house and restored it to its present state. The restoration work was performed under the supervision of Raiford Stripling and Ray R. Stripling, architects, and the carpenters were Ray Bennefield and Louis Runnels. At that time, the Clarks gave the property the name of Straddlefork Farm after the nearby country store which served the community and was located at the fork of Farm Road 705 and State Highway 147.

The property was originally settled by Jacob Herring in 1836, during the early days of the Republic of Texas. Jacob Herring was known as a stalwart, sturdy citizen who minded his own affairs, lived at peace with his neighbors, and won the regard of his fellowmen by his kindliness and just dealings. Herring's original house was east of the present site across Farm Road 705. The present house was constructed in 1875 from timbers taken from the original Herring house. The design is typical of the unpretentious country homes of that period. Built on the familiar dogtrot plan, a central hallway runs through the house, and fireplaces at the ends fo the two front rooms provide heat. A gallery onto which the three front doors open runs across the entire front of the house and is covered by the extended roof.

All of the floors and the hand-planed ceilings are of heart pine. Pediment trim crowns the doors and windows, and the front rooms boast molded wood wainscots. In the rear are shed rooms which have lower ceilings than the front rooms.

Behind the house is an enormous pecan tree. Its unusual size is reputedly explained by the story that one of Jacob Herring's daughters planted it in an abandoned well.

THE J. SIMP MILLER HOUSE
(3 miles south on Farm Road 2213)

Leroy Miller, the father of J. Simp Miller, came to Texas from Alabama in the early part of the nineteenth century. Shortly after his arrival in Texas, he married Tryphenia Crawford, daughter of Jacob Crawford. Leroy Miller was a charter member of the McFarland Masonic Lodge in San Augustine.

J. Simp Miller was born in 1853 and later inherited the land for his homestead from his father. The Simp Miller house was constructed by the carpenter, Duncan Crisp, in about 1875. J. Simp Miller was a farmer, stock raiser, and owner of a cotton gin. Miller Mathews, Simp Miller's grandson, remembers his farm as a self-sustaining operation with a commissary, gristmill, gin, sawmill and quarters for the tenant workers.

The Simp Miller house is interesting architecturally for its clean-lined cornice treatment and "profile" porch railings. The present owner is Miller Mathews of San Augustine.

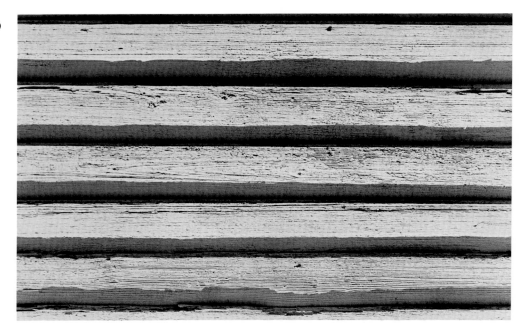

THE KETCHUM PLACE
(1018 Milam Street)

ABEL COFFIN KETCHUM was born in Pennsylvania in 1849 and came to Texas with his family while still an infant. At the time of the Civil War, the family resided in Sabine Pass, where Ketchum grew up to be a ship's carpenter like his father before him. Because the coast did not appeal to his wife, Ketchum moved to San Augustine and decided to build houses instead of ships.

Mrs. Elsie M. Norvell, who resides in the Ketchum place and is the present owner, writes of Ketchum, "He built the Presbyterian Church and did a lot of work on the Methodist Church. He was Superintendent of the Methodist Sunday School for many years and was loved by all who knew him. He built a sailboat for himself named the *Tom & Abel*. He was a duly licensed Captain, and made trips to New York in his vessel and numerous coastwise trips for transporting freight. There are many homes in San Augustine that he built, and they are a monument to his memory. He died at the age of 90."

Ketchum's house which was completed in 1879, was built along the same lines and durability of a ship. This unique structure is one of the first split-level houses of the era and has 4 X 4 inch studding and bracing throughout the main part of the house. The house is built of heart pine (most of it hand-planed), and unusual hand-carved scrolls decorate the fireplace mantel. The Ketchum place is a superb example of fine craftsmanship and pleasing simplicity in a small house.

HORATIO M. HANKS HOUSE
(State Highway 21)

ON THE BAYOU, one block north of the present crossing on Highway 21, three miles south of San Augustine, is located the Hanks residence. Wyatt Hanks and his brothers, James and Horatio, came to Texas from Indiana County, Kentucky, in March, 1826. Hanks applied for land in Stephen F. Austin's colony on July 1, 1826, but failed to secure a homestead there. He and his brothers then located in the Ayish Bayou settlement. Hanks built a saw-and-gristmill three miles south of San Augustine and later represented the Ayish Bayou in the Convention of 1832. He continued to operate his mill until November, 1834, when he was granted land in Zavala's colony near the present town of Jasper. During the Texas Revolution in 1836, he was quartermaster of the Jasper volunteers, but the group failed to reach Sam Houston's army in time to participate in the Battle of San Jacinto.

Wyatt Hanks, Argalus Parker, and John R. Bevil were involved in one of the early East Texas feuds relating to land frauds. After the killing of several men on each side, Hanks left Jasper and settled on Wolf Creek in Tyler County. Hanks was a member of the family from which the mother of Abraham Lincoln came. It is said that he received a letter from Lincoln before the Civil War advising him to sell his slaves. Hanks, who was an ardent advocate of the Southern cause, was so indignant on receiving such an abolitionist letter, that he threw it into the fire. Undoubtedly, the family would have given a great deal for the letter after Lincoln became president.

The Horatio M. Hanks home was built in 1880 and today remains in good condition. The double chimneys off-center from the main rooms help make the house interesting architecturally. The house is now owned by Mrs. Raymond Young, who bought it from the Hanks family in 1931.

McRAE PRESBYTERIAN CHURCH
(4 miles west off State Highway 21)

IN 1882, the Reverend D. A. McRae organized the McRae Presbyterian Church five miles west of San Augustine for the members of his congregation who lived in that neighborhood. The building, which was erected by the church members in one day, has lumber pre-cut by Captain T. W. Blount's field hands.

The Reverend Mr. McRae came to San Augustine in May of 1880; he served his congregation for forty years and was a most devout and tireless servant of the Lord. Mr. McRae died in 1920 and was buried in the cemetery adjoining the church.

While regular services are no longer held in the church, there is an annual homecoming each summer.

THE NEWT WHITTON HOUSE
(In New Hope Community, 8 miles NW off State Highway 21)

WILLIAM NEWTON WHITTON, known to all as Newt Whitton, was born in Georgia in 1846. Whitton served in the Confederate Army, then moved to San Augustine and in 1870 received an appointment from the governor as surveyor of San Augustine County. Whitton did not consider himself competent enough at that time for appointment to the office, so he declined the offer and continued to practice surveying on his father's farm. In 1871, the appointment was again offered, and this time he accepted.

In the book, *Father Wore Gray*, by Lela Whitton Hegarty, published in 1963, Whitton's daughter writes of the obstacles a surveyor such as her father confronted: "The county was wilderness in those days. There were dense forests, jungles, and cane brakes, wild cats, and varmints of all kinds. There were clouds of buffalo gnats, and mosquitoes, ticks, and snakes seemed to be everywhere. He (Whitton) had to wear heavy clothing, high boots, leather pants, two pistols and carry a thirty pound compass in summer and winters.

"The legislature passed a law requiring all land certificates to be located, surveyed and returned to the land office on or before January 1, 1875. This meant hardship for county surveyors. Mr. Whitton carried a tent and camping equipment to areas where he had to stay several days or weeks. In his crew he had a cook, a hunter to kill wild game, ax-men to cut the underbrush on the line to be surveyed, a pack of hounds, and chain men to measure the land. Many times he had to survey in sleet and snow with icy timber falling around him. At night, he wrote field notes by the camp fire sitting at a homemade folding table and folding chair."

Mr. Whitton married Mary Elizabeth Yarbrough in 1884, and shortly thereafter, began building his home on his Blue Creek farm near Denning.

When completed, the house had five rooms and a kitchen ten feet away which was connected to the main house by a covered walkway. The house was painted white and had one brick chimney. Later, the Whitton family added two more rooms and another chimney to the original structure. The workmanship throughout is very skilled.

Mrs. Daphine Whitton Winkler, of Bossier City, Louisiana, a daughter of German Whitton, now owns the Newt Whitton house.

THE BODINE PLACE
(4 miles north on State Highway 147, then 2 miles west)

THE structure standing at present was built in 1886 and is the third house built by the Bodine family on this site. The house contains a fine mantel with hand-carved, fluted Ionic columns removed from an older house in San Augustine.

The original builder was John Bodine, a soldier and prestigious sailor who served under Commodore Oliver Hazard Perry on Lake Erie in 1812. John Bodine named his son for that officer, and one son in each succeeding generation has been named Oliver Hazard Perry Bodine in memory of the Commodore. The owner of the Bodine house is Tom Bodine, a descendant of John Bodine.

THE "YELLOW HOUSE" & HOLLIS BUILDING
(128 East Columbia)

WHEN the town of San Augustine was a frontier and the politics of the Republic were actively being pursued, an immense house known as the "Yellow House" was occupied by John P. Border who was a soldier in the Battle of San Jacinto, colonel of a Confederate regiment, and later clerk of the District Court of San Augustine County. Border was in the mercantile business and on this site he and Sebastian Francois operated as partners in one of the early businesses of the town. In later years, John C. Deyle used the "Yellow House" as a bakery, until the building was moved across the street to provide room for business houses.

In 1884, I. H. Hollis purchased the lot where the "Yellow House" was and built a two-story brick structure with wooden floors, divided off-center by a stairway to the upper floor. The small portion of the lower floor, known as the corner division, has successively housed a "Pharmocotherapia," a U. S. Post

Office, and a grocery. The larger portion was used as a mercantile store.

On the upper floor the years have seen established the first telephone exchange in San Augustine, an insurance office, and a doctor's office. The larger portion of the upper story was used by the townspeople as a ballroom where the young people of the town danced during the twenties and thirties; later it served as office for the Farm Home Administration.

The San Augustine Historical Society describes the building as it stands today: "The present renovation of the building is unique in that the bricks were sand blasted; the awnings are supported by French metal posts; and the interior has been reclaimed, leaving the high metal ceilings; and the original iron and steel frame supports were left in their original visible state, giving a New Orleans effect and preserving the architecture of the 1890s. This building incidentally, is one of the few buildings remaining in town after the great fire of 1890."

The old Hollis building is now owned by Mr. and Mrs. John Oglesbee, Jr., of San Augustine.

THE GATLING HOUSE
(South Liberty Street)

THE information on the Gatling home was provided by the late Mrs. Mary Gatling Blount, daughter of George Edward Gatling, builder and owner of the Gatling house: "George Edward Gatling, a Confederate veteran, and first cousin of the inventor of the Gatling gun, came to Texas in 1869 from North Carolina. He came into San Augustine over the El Camino Real on an ox wagon and was impressed by the natural beauty of the surrounding country. He looked no further and decided to adopt San Augustine as his future home. He practiced law and served as County Attorney, also acting as special Judge from time to time. In the Masonic Lodge, he served as Worshipful Master. His special interest was establishing land titles and making an abstract of the lands in the County.

"In 1886 he married Miss Cynthia Massey, whose parents had come to Texas in 1837 from Tennessee. Two years later he bought seventy acres, and hired the carpenter, Thad Caldwell, to build his home on South Liberty Street. This home was built of lumber cut from virgin pine heart timber, and the lumber is as sound today as when it was first used in 1889. The hand-hewn sills were 6 X 12 inches, the walls were of rough 1 X 12 inch boxing planks both inside and outside with 1 X 6 inch outside covering and the paneled ceilings were of hand-planed batten boards. There are two single chimneys and one double chimney between the kitchen and bedroom which provide heat for the house; these chimneys were built of hand-molded brick. The sides and backs of the fireplaces were made of large blocks of native rock cut by hand to fit the openings. The double chimney furnishes heat for the kitchen today as it did in 1889. The house was built on a hilltop near a hillside sloping down to a small ravine which makes a picturesque scene. It was the plan of my parents to preserve the natural beauty of the site and make the home more attractive by the use of the native trees and shrubs."

The home is now owned by Mary Gatling Blount's daughter and her husband, Mr. and Mrs. D. E. Bailey of Beaumont. They have restored the home and grounds in keeping with George Gatling's design by landscaping with redbuds, dogwoods, and magnolias.

The home has been owned continuously by the Gatling family, and as such it is furnished with the accumulated antiques of four generations. A number of pieces have been in the family since 1840. There is a collection of pressed and satin glass, with a number of signed pieces. One bowl is signed 1853, and one light fixture is inscribed July 9, 1862. The mantel in the living room is of carved cherry wood on top of which rests a mirror that reaches to the ceiling. Mrs. Blount adds, "There is no claim to greatness, just a home that holds a place in the hearts of the Gatling Family, and they wish to show their love by placing a Historical Medallion on the House."

BROOKELAND DEPOT
(Attoyac Farm, west via State Highway 21 on Farm Road 1196)

CHARLES WOODBURN, president of the Texas State Historical Survey Committee wrote: "There is a lot of nostalgia to be connected with the old depot. Passenger depots, once the center of community life in small cities and towns, have been boarded up, torn down or converted to other uses and are fast disappearing from the Texas scene."

The Brookeland Depot, now located outside of San Augustine, is at least one exception to this. The depot was constructed in 1914 to handle heavy lumber movements of the John Henry Kirby lumber and oil empire. Kirby was the organizer of the Great Northern Railway which ran through Brookeland Depot. Shortly after the formative years of Kirby's business enterprises, the Santa Fe Railway took over the operation of both his railroads and of Brookeland Depot.

In 1960, when the Sam Rayburn Dam was being built, the Great Northern Railway relocated and the 1914 depot was declared surplus. Mr. and Mrs. Ray H. Horton of Houston, previous recipients of the Texas Preservation Award, bought the depot and moved it forty miles to their Attoyac Farm where it was painstakingly restored to its original atmosphere. It is presently used as a farmhouse.

The Brookeland Depot was awarded an official Texas Historical Medallion with interpretive plate on April 6, 1967.

BIBLIOGRAPHY

Books:

Alexander, Drury. *Texas Homes of the 19th Century.* Austin & London: University of Texas Press, 1966.

Bracken, Dorothy K., and Maurine Whorton Redway. *Early Texas Homes.* Dallas: Southern Methodist University Press, 1966.

Crocket, George L. *An Historical Sketch.* Unpublished manuscript.

Crocket, George L. *Two Centuries in East Texas.* Dallas: The Southwest Press, 1932.

Hegarty, Lela Whitton. *Father Wore Grey.* San Antonio: Naylor Publishing Co., 1963.

Johnson, F. W. *Texas and Texans,* Vols. I, II, III, IV. Updated by Eugene C. Barker. Chicago & New York: American Historical Society, 1914.

Oberste, Monseigneur William H. *The Restless Friar.* Austin: Von-Boeckmann Jones, 1970.

Webb, Walter Prescott, ed. *The Handbook of Texas,* Vols. I, II. Austin: Texas State Historical Association, 1952.

Pamphlets:

Morning Worship Program, 129th Anniversary Service. San Augustine, Texas: Memorial Presbyterian Church, June 4, 1967.

San Augustine County Development Association. *San Augustine, "the Cradle of Texas."* Diboll, Texas: The Free Press, n. d.

San Augustine, "the Cradle of Texas." San Augustine, Texas: Daughters of the Republic of Texas, 1968.

Seale, William. *San Augustine in the Texas Republic.* Austin: The Encino Press, 1969.

Texas State Historical Survey Committee. *Guide to Official Texas Historical Markers.* Austin: Texas Historical Foundation, 1971.

Newspaper:

Holbrook, Raymond. " 'Retirement' Means Oblivion for Most Old Railroad Cars." *Dallas Morning News,* August 1, 1966.

INTERVIEWS AND ACKNOWLEDGEMENTS

Individuals:

Mrs. Mary Landon Blount Bailey, Beaumont
Mrs. E. B. Bittick, San Augustine
Mr. and Mrs. Edward Clark, San Augustine
Mr. and Mrs. C. T. Dorsey, San Augustine
Dr. and Mrs. Curtis Haley, San Augustine
Harlowe W. Johnson, San Augustine
Miller Matthews, San Augustine
Charles Sharp McMillan, San Augustine
Mrs. Elsie Norvell, San Augustine
Mr. Jack Osborne, Beaumont
Mr. Will Partin, San Augustine
Ben Ramsey, San Augustine
C. S. Ramsey, San Augustine
Walter Smith, San Augustine
Raiford Stripling, San Augustine
Mr. W. J. Teel, San Augustine County Judge
Mrs. Nelsyn Wade, San Augustine
Mrs. W. M. Wade, San Augustine
Julian Whitton, San Augustine

Organization:

The San Augustine Historical Society